ADDICTED

to an

ADDICT

Your Life Matters

START PUTTING YOUR ENERGY, TIME AND EFFORT INTO CREATING THE LIFE YOU DESERVE

GW00771954

SUNA SPRY RSPH

NLP PRACTITIONER & CERTIFIED LIFE COACH

Cover image by: Sam Arts Studio
Book design by: SWATT Books Ltd

Printed in the United Kingdom
First Printing, 2021

ISBN: 978-1-8383258-0-0 (Paperback)
ISBN: 978-1-8383258-1-7 (eBook)

Suna Spry
London
SE9 4RP

CONTENTS

Introduction   5

Seven Truths About Addicts   9

My Story   15

PART 1   21

Facing Reality   21

The Love Language   27

Standards and Boundaries   35

The Magic Question   39

PART 2   41

Taking Action   41

PART 3   79

Learning to Fly   79

Gratitude   95

INTRODUCTION

This book is for all those who love and care for an addict.

Firstly, congratulations on realising that you are enough, and that you are worthy of living the life you deserve, and also for purchasing this book.

Are you prepared to accept your true feelings and needs? Are you ready to face up to what, until now, you might not have realised, or were unwilling to admit has been happening in your relationship and life with an addict? If so, this book will allow you to take that important initial step towards your dreams, goals and desires, as you begin to understand that your life truly matters, too.

Each section of this book will provide you with deep insights into addiction, while explaining how you can start working on **YOU** by preparing to take action and learning how to start living the life of freedom and clarity that you deserve.

Are you consumed by an addict and their addictions? Addiction can manifest as behaviour ranging from dependence on substances such as **drugs** or **alcohol**, to obsession with **sex, porn, gambling, social media, chat rooms, food, smoking** and even **dating**. There are many others that I could also mention, but I think you're getting the picture.

Chances are, you genuinely love the addict in your life, and so maybe you do not want to leave them, but you have now tried everything to get them clean and sober, or weaned off whatever their particular vice may be, without success.

What would your life be like if you knew exactly how to handle this disease? What if you knew how to deal with all the **lies, broken promises** and **blame?**

Imagine feeling peace of mind about your future, rediscovering your courage and confidence, and having a major breakthrough in your relationship. **Is it possible?**

This book will give you the tools and strategies that you need to stop being consumed by issues outside your control. It will orientate you towards action, growth and the realisation of your dreams.

You will come to accept that if you decide to stay with the addict, you will not be able to fix or control them. As the saying goes, you can lead a horse to water, but you cannot make it drink. The addict must arrive at the realisation that they have a problem on their own. Only then can they utilise help and support.

Are you ready to become a better version of yourself?

In Part 1, you will learn seven truths about addicts, and complete the first in a series of exercises that will enhance each stage of your learning. These exercises are designed to help you clarify exactly what it is that you desire from life, while also opening your eyes to the truth of what is happening around you, giving you the freedom to stop carrying the addict.

You might have already tried some of the following suggestions in the past, such as refusing to talk, suppressing your feelings or trying to stay positive, and while these may seem like coping mechanisms, they are actually effective methods for avoiding traps that feed into a trauma system. To take control of your life, you first need to face the issue, the source of your pain, and admit to yourself that you cannot fix them, as anything else will only delay your long overdue healing.

So, are you ready to start working on YOU?

INTRODUCTION

SEVEN TRUTHS ABOUT ADDICTS

I was that person once, struggling every day to support my parent / friend / partner / spouse / family member.

Each day would be the same: how would they come home? I could always smell it first; always that same smell, same look, same aggression and same attitude. I would instantly become anxious, as I wondered if they were going to be happy, sad or angry after their eight pints, packet of cocaine or cannabis joint. I would worry in case the internet connection played up, as this could seriously impact how the day went, and then there was the constant eating and cravings for sugar.

Thankfully, I don't live that life anymore, as I am no longer defined by an addicted person's behaviour. I have learned how to identify my true purpose, embracing what makes me truly happy while controlling the fear, stress, anxiety, sadness, hurt and anger that once consumed me. This has enabled me to become more positive and fulfilled than ever before.

How addictions form

Addiction is often the result of childhood experiences that haven't been fully processed or resolved, although this is not always the case.

There are many types of addiction, eg to substances such as **tobacco, drugs** and **alcohol**, or activities such as **gambling, shopping**, and **browsing the internet**. When a person has experienced any form of abuse, be it physical, sexual or mental, it could later manifest as a downward spiral into addiction.

The human brain evolved into its modern form over the course of thousands of years, but its two primary functions have always remained the same:

- To seek out pleasure
- To avoid pain

In prehistoric times, avoiding pain would have meant finding shelter, hunting and gathering food to avoid starvation, and protecting one's self by maintaining a constant state of vigilance against potential attacks.

Although our modern world is very different from that of our ancient ancestors, our basic brain configuration hasn't really changed. We are still wired to seek out **PLEASURE** and avoid **PAIN**.

As humanity has evolved, so too has our ability to create and consume all manner of addictive substances, including **refined sugar, alcohol, nicotine, cannabis, cocaine, and convenience foods**. Even though we sometimes know that we are overindulging to the point of dependence or long-term personal detriment, our brains are so hardwired to the pursuit of pleasure that we find ourselves unable to stop.

Seven truths about addicts

1. When we consume something addictive (eg nicotine), our brain and body will crave it for as long as it is in our system. Addictive substances connect to our internal safety mechanisms, much like food and water, tricking our subconscious mind into believing that these products are essential for survival, regardless of all evidence to the contrary. Thus, our inner-self develops primal urges that may cause physical and mental withdrawal symptoms as the substance leaves the body, such as stomach cramps, mood swings or hot sweats.

2. The addict's subconscious mind does not want to be cut off from the source of pleasure. When the addict consumes whatever it is that they are craving, feelings of anxiety and emptiness start to fade as withdrawal symptoms subside. This is how addiction patterns are formed.

3. When an addict says that they can go without the source of their addiction for a day, a week or even a month, they may be telling the truth. However, they will not be able to rid themselves of cravings until they are able to alter their underlying mental state, as although the initial decision to take an addictive substance is made consciously, it becomes a case of the subconscious dictating usage after only the third or fourth occasion.

4. A person who struggles with addiction is also likely to suffer with mental health issues and physical ailments, both short-term and chronically.

5. There are many signs of addiction that may be evident to others:

   - Frequently appearing intoxicated.
   - Developing issues with cognition and memory.
   - Being lethargic, sleeping more, sleeping irregular hours and appearing unwell or tired.
   - Getting into trouble at work or school.
   - Attending social events only if drugs or alcohol are available; becoming intoxicated before the social event, or declining to attend in order to drink or use drugs alone.
   - Neglecting personal hygiene.
   - Displaying symptoms of a nervous disposition (eg ticks, stutters, etc).

6. Substance addicts are likely to behave differently while intoxicated than if sober. When intoxicated, they may say or do **hurtful things** and become **violent** or **abusive**. They may t**ake control of money**, **neglect** family and friends, **tell lies** and be generally **deceitful**, perhaps seeking extramarital **affairs**. They may become **depressed** and **lose self-confidence**, potentially leading to acts of **self-sabotage** that could see them seriously risk their own lives as well as others' (eg **driving while intoxicated**).

7. Although it is not always their intention, addicts will often make others feel fearful by assigning blame for their behaviour instead of taking responsibility. Within their flawed frame of logic, there is always an excuse for any transgression, and this will not change unless

they are willing to admit to themselves that they have a problem and are in need of support. This is centrally important to your own healing, as there is nothing you can do to help them until they reach this point, and it is only through wholehearted acceptance of this fact that you will discover if you have become addicted to the addict and created a relationship of co-dependence.

SEVEN TRUTHS ABOUT ADDICTS

MY STORY

I was born in London Middlesex Hospital in 1967, to a Scottish lady and Turkish-Cypriot man who had been trying to conceive for seven years.

I had my first experience of sexual abuse at the age of seven, which came at the hands of a family member. At the time, I was too young to understand that what was happening to me was wrong, and so I went along with my abuser's insistence that it remain 'our little secret.' This period marked my introduction to the feeling of being entirely alone in the world, and having no one to turn to for help.

During the 1960s and '70s, my father was a successful businessman around the popular Soho district of London, where he ran cabaret clubs frequented by the likes of the infamous Krays twins. My parents divorced when I was three years old, and I soon became a 'once every other weekend' child, splitting my time between two households, neither of which were ideal environments for an infant. It was around this time that my mother became an alcoholic, leading to a cycle of neglect that left me relying on myself for basic care, while simultaneously exposing me as an easy target for her verbal abuse. As an adult, I am able to understand and empathise with the challenges she was facing at that point in her life, and I have since forgiven her, but this does not change the fact that many of my formative years were lost to another person's addiction.

My mother and I moved house several times during my childhood, as she attempted to lay down roots and start afresh, and when, after spending time in a battered women's hostel, we were eventually assigned a permanent residence by the local authority, we finally had a place to call home. Having at last achieved some sense of stability, I secretly began to hope that my mother's drinking would stop and our life would improve, but the situation only went from bad to worse as she started a relationship that quickly became violent. The result was that whenever she experienced violence herself, she would become more abusive and on occasions violent towards me.

A ray of sunlight appeared when I was seven and a half, with the arrival of my adorable younger sister. However, my joy at finally having someone to be close to and love was soon tempered by the escalating abuse and violence at home. Then, one day, a woman arrived to see my mother, and we suddenly packed up and left the flat. We were taken to another location, a long distance away, where spent a few months in what I now realise was another battered women's hostel. My memories of this time are very vivid; I can recall exactly how I felt while living in the hostel. I retreated into myself, not communicating much if at all, and I also started to wet the bed, which led to a buzzer being attached to the mattress. Whenever I'd begin to urinate in my sleep, it would buzz loudly and wake me up, causing great humiliation as the entire floor would know what had happened.

After what felt like a long time, we were again assigned a flat by the local authority. I was now eight and a half years old, and the bulk of my days were spent looking after my sister. I taught myself how to run a house, learning to cook for both myself and my sister, and so one positive, if you could frame it in such a way, was that I developed many important life skills. I also started to go out and play with the new friends I made at school, and although I mostly had to take my sister along in her pushchair, she was happy enough to be left on the swings while I spent time with my friends.

I wasn't the only one making friends in our new neighbourhood; my mother became close to a woman whose seventeen-year-old daughter began grooming me along with her nineteen-year-old boyfriend. They each took turns abusing me, presenting it as a kind of perverted game, and because my only means of self-preservation was to lock these terrible memories away in a box at the back of my mind, I'm not even able to describe what either of them looked like.

I left home at the age of seventeen and moved in with my boyfriend, who was twenty-three. I was eight months pregnant with his child when he first started to beat me up, and I would be forced to lock myself in the bathroom to escape. I was so scared of him that all I did was cry and cry, as I asked myself what I had done to deserve it; my thoughts drifting between wondering why he didn't love me and dreading the next beating. There were times during this period where I thought about taking my own life, but my newborn son gave me the strength to carry on.

I was still very young and naïve back then, and so I hadn't spotted the early warning signs that my son's father was an alcoholic, even though I had seen it all before with my mother. By that point, all I could think about was protecting my child by finding us somewhere safe to live, but at the same I felt completely trapped. In the end, after two years, I took my son and fled to a homeless centre, where I had to show evidence of abuse by having a doctor measure and document my bruises (this was before the proliferation of camera phones).

The following three years were spent rebuilding my life, during which time I was assigned a permanent residence to call home, and I eventually went on to meet my future husband, with whom I had two more children. We set out on what appeared to be a mostly nice, happy life together, until I came to realise that he was addicted to cocaine and had been cheating on me with another woman. He was also susceptible to get-rich-quick schemes, which led to him wasting the money that I was responsible for providing, causing me to lose all trust in him. I was utterly devastated at this turn of events, and I began to wonder if it was my fault that men continued to treat me so poorly. I felt like a perennial victim, forever asking myself, *Why me?*

Following the breakup of my marriage, I started a relationship with another man who turned out to be a cocaine addict, and I couldn't help but suspect that I must have 'DRUGS ARE HERE' tattooed on my forehead. The realisation that I had attracted yet another addict was too much to bear; I couldn't take it anymore. I was on the verge of a nervous breakdown, and so I made the decision to go and live in Egypt for a year. I felt angry, depressed and lacking in self-belief, and I knew that I had to get away from it all. I had no faith in men or my own judgement, I couldn't stop crying and my self-esteem was in tatters. Time and time again, I had been let down by the people who should have been looking out for me, and I felt so alone in the world that I became consumed by disgust and resentment towards everything that had happened in my life. I didn't understand why I couldn't have a relationship free of addiction or abuse, and I was tormented by questions about why I could never be enough for someone.

MY STORY

After living in Egypt and meeting some truly amazing people, who helped me come to terms with my struggles and taught me about spirituality, as well as how to look deep within myself and connect to my heart, I started to break down the mental barriers that I had put up to protect myself. This allowed me to begin to see the good that existed inside of myself and in my life, as I finally found a way to appreciate my true worth and value as a human being. I returned to Britain a completely different person; I was no longer the victim, and I was not responsible for the cycle of addiction and abuse that I had been born into. I had done a lot of soul-searching during my time abroad, finding that through confronting my own limiting beliefs I had gained the power to truly **love** and **appreciate** myself for the first time. I was, and always had been, **enough**.

I have since discovered my calling in life: to help and support others who care for and love an addict. They are the victims of addiction for whom there exists no network of support, despite the fact that their lives are often taken over by the needs of another. I know this because throughout all of my experiences with addicts, I was never able to secure any help for myself (I did receive years of counselling for the other abuses I have suffered, but living with an addict is a different kind of animal). This inspired me to set-up **Visions & Dreams**, which uses one-to-one coaching as a method of supporting and guiding people through difficult times, and includes a three-stage programme for anyone facing the challenge of loving and caring for an addict. It also provides advice on nutrition and weight management, with a view to avoiding the temptation of comfort eating, as well as support for those going through the menopause or experiencing bereavement. In my quest to develop a comprehensive, holistic approach to the well-being of the mind, body and soul, I have become a qualified celebrant and positive physiologist, in addition to receiving licences to practise both hypnotherapy and neurolinguistic programming (NLP). After years of study and research to complement my own experiences of caring for and loving an addict, I now support and guide others as they navigate the same path I once walked, empowering them to live the life that they deserve and desire.

Although much of my focus is directed at helping others, I still find time to work on myself each and every day. I continue to recite affirmations and write in my journal, meditating over and manifesting whatever it is that I truly want. This enables me to live the life that I deserve and desire – and, most importantly of all, to have my freedom – and you can experience this sense of liberation, too. Affirmations are a great way of practising positive thought and self-empowerment, as they foster the belief that a concentrated mindset can lead to success in every walk of life. In my journal, I record all of my thoughts for the day, and wherever negative emotions appear, I look for ways to transform them into positives by using them as opportunities for personal growth.

I try to meditate most days, although it is not always possible when life gets in the way, as meditation trains the mind to focus and redirect thoughts. You may utilise this ancient technique as a means of increasing your awareness of yourself and your surroundings, with many practitioners seeing it as a way to reduce stress and increase concentration levels. Another discipline that is great for honing both the mind and body, and which has enjoyed an explosion in popularity in recent years, is yoga.

'Love yourself as much as
you want to be loved.'

Part 1

FACING REALITY

If you love and care for an addict, yours will be a long and excruciating road towards acceptance that there is absolutely nothing you can do to change what is happening.

**'When you're exhausted, heartbroken...
when you feel the pain of their self-
destruction consuming you.'**

The relationships and the world around you will start to break, and you will feel totally alone, and that is when you'll know in the deepest and purest part of yourself that you just can't live like this anymore.

When you love an addict, learning how to face reality is the most important first step towards **surviving**. Although it may *seem* easier to stay in the **fantasy space**, where you can continue to believe that things are going to magically get better, you need to face the fact that there is no such magic. Things will not simply get better on their own just because you wish that they would; this is going to take a lot of hard work and effort.

In this situation, coming face-to-face with reality means accepting that parts of your life might have gotten out of control as a result of you loving someone who is engaging in addictive behaviours.

Are you absorbed in someone else's addiction?

Have you 'let yourself go?' Have you gained weight and stopped making time for your friends? Is your work life suffering? Would you like to experience new things, such as studying professionally or academically, or practising yoga? Would you like to find a new job or change career paths? Perhaps you have always wanted to start a business?

You may be feeling a constant, gnawing worry that you live with every day. You may often find yourself being asked for money, and feel guilty for saying no. Perhaps you are watching everything you say and do in order to **keep the peace** at home, for fear of making the addict angry; walking on eggshells rather than expressing yourself freely. You may be asked to do favours for the addict on a consistent basis, such as watching their children or running their errands. You may not know how to say no to them, but you have to start putting **YOU** first and recognise that this is not the way to lead a healthy life or be your best self.

You are a beautiful person with real value and so much to offer, but it doesn't always feel that way when you share your life with an addict. Addicts often make you feel rotten about yourself, and unworthy of love. You may feel wrapped up in shame, or dark and depressed due to the trauma of loving someone suffering from addiction.

Whatever your particular situation is,
acceptance of what you are dealing
with is the first survival tip for anyone
loving and caring for an addict.

QUESTIONNAIRE

Read through the following questions and answer what is true for you. Remember that you honour your intuition by not overthinking a question and allowing the truth to emerge organically, so try to answer as quickly as possible.

————————

1. Has your partner ever tried to stop you from seeing your friends or family?

   _____

   _____

2. Has your partner ever prevented you from studying or going to work?

   _____

   _____

3. Does your partner constantly check up on you or follow you?

   _____

   _____

4. Does your partner constantly humiliate or criticise you when they are drunk?

   _____

   _____

5. Does your partner accuse you of flirting or having affairs?

   _____

   _____

6. Are you ever afraid of your partner, or afraid what they may do to themselves?

   _____

   _____

7. Has your partner ever deliberately destroyed your belongings?

   _____

   _____

8. Has your partner ever made you get into a car that they have then driven while under the influence of alcohol and / or drugs?

   _____

   _____

9. Does your partner control your finances, leaving you short of money for shopping and essentials, or even without money for yourself and your children?

   _____

   _____

10. Has your partner ever forced you to do something that you really didn't want to do?

   _____

   _____

If you have answered yes to one or more of the above questions, you may be consumed by and / or co-dependent on an addict.

FACING REALITY

THE LOVE LANGUAGE

In a relationship with an addict, long days and busy schedules will often cause love to fall by the wayside, making it likely that you have forgotten how it feels to be complimented or embraced, or what it means to experience any of those little things that say '**I love you.**' This is because the addict is so consumed by their own negative, inward-facing struggles and addictive behaviour that they simply do not have the capacity to pay attention to you. There's also the possibility that they are deliberately starving you of love, in order to make you appreciate it when you do finally receive some much-needed affection.

Initially, an addicted person may appear just as fun and exciting, and loving and caring, as anyone else. They'll use all five love language techniques: words of affirmation, physical touch, giving gifts, spending quality time and engaging in acts of service, and it may be the case that you only discover their addiction once it is already too late to reverse course, as you have fallen in love and committed yourself emotionally, or become entangled through shared living arrangements. This is a common situation for a **Love Addict** to find themselves in (ie someone who doesn't feel fulfilled unless they are in a relationship), as this type of person usually attracts **Love Avoidants** (either an addict or someone who was smothered and / or controlled with affection as a child).

A history of abandonment, neglect or inadequate / inconsistent nurturing often leads to love addiction, as attachment patterns developed during a child's first 18 months will serve to inform how a person gives and receives care. By focussing their energy onto someone else, the love addict suppresses their own pain and trauma, but this only causes childhood issues to fester and grow into adult problems. As a result, the love addict may choose to stay in a relationship with a love avoidant, believing that by helping them to overcome their addiction, they will 'fix' the situation and make the relationship stronger. However, the reality is that the love addict now becomes addicted to the idea of 'saving' the love avoidant.

The more involved the love addict becomes, the more vicious the cycle of disappointment and anger gets, until eventually it breaks down and then starts all over again, as the avoidant tells the addict what they know they want to hear: **'I love you... I'm sorry... I will try harder... Let me take you out... Let me treat you...'** The avoidant will even offer to get help for their own addiction, but this will only ever amount to a brief period of respite before the relationship deteriorates once again.

> **'A person can apologise endlessly, and even if you forgive them, sometimes you can't forget the pain they've cause you.'**

When the addict we love is also a relative, it can be even more difficult than dealing with an addicted partner, as we may feel as though there is no walking away from family bonds. If the addict is our child or parent, we may believe that we should simply accept their behaviour, due to what is defined and taught to us as **'unconditional love,'** but the truth is that what we often refer to as **'tough love'** may be more effective in helping an addict to recover. Tough love may involve drawing very definite, non-negotiable boundaries, or perhaps going so far as having a clean break from an addict.

LOVE SHOULD ALWAYS START WITH YOU!

Conflict with an addict

So, your partner has once again embarrassed you in front of people, and now you're all riled up and ready to explode. You're angry, hurt and disappointed; you begin to nag and moan, as your body language screams that you're ready for a fight. You make accusations and give lectures, and your partner promises not to do it again, but you have every right to feel aggrieved, as another thread in the rope that's keeping you attached is broken. They become defensive and deny any wrongdoing, which gets your back up even more, and now they're lashing out and refusing to accept responsibility. They're trying to deflect the blame back onto you, pushing you down into a lower mood – 'I have proof! I have witnesses!' – as they attempt to wrestle back control of the narrative through name-calling. They resort to throwing your past in your face, even though it has nothing to do with their behaviour, and when that doesn't work they change tactics and start saying all the things that they know you want to hear. You keep going around in circles until you reach the point where they're ready to try manipulating you, which may play out as them using the incident as an excuse to feed their addiction. This sets the whole process in motion yet again, leaving you feeling like crap and racked with self-doubt as you ask yourself over and over, *Is it me?*

I am a feisty person, and so these situations would often get me fired up (being an Aries doesn't help!), but you may be a person who does not enjoy confrontation, which leads to you just shutting up and allowing another outburst to be swept under the carpet. This only contributes to the same old vicious cycle that leaves you clinging to a connection that isn't really there, as you seek to justify your own addiction to the addict. The strong feelings that arise from conflict with your partner are nothing but temporary flickers of emotion, and thus not a suitable foundation to build on. All you're doing is contriving ways to feel a sense of agency in a situation that is, by its very nature, out of control.

I used to record what the addict would say to me. I know it sounds strange, but I had to do something to confirm to myself that I was not going mad, and that the problem was not me. Eventually, I was able to see that it wasn't normal for me to be having to gather evidence just to prove to myself that I am not some villain, which helped me resolve to stop wasting my time and energy on the addict.

Here's something to remember: feeling embarrassed by other people's actions or behaviours (or even your own) is a sign of co-dependency.

'Living with fear, resentment and a broken heart is not how you deserve to live.'

Fighting can be a natural part of a healthy relationship, as can feelings of anger and sadness, but this only works as long as both people share the same goal. In a relationship where two people are working towards conflicting ends (eg one is an addict in denial about their addiction), one side needs to drop any expectation that the other will ever compromise in order to find common ground. You will not be able to form a healthy relationship with an addict until they take responsibility for themselves and commit to long-term sobriety (there are many support groups available for those who are ready to take this step), and while I am not saying that you should leave your addict if they fail to do this, it is important for you to know that you have a choice.

Whatever decision you come to is perfectly fine; there is no judgement here. I am simply letting you know that there is support for you no matter what. You do not need to carry on suffering alone.

If you love someone with addiction, you are not powerless in the matter, nor do you have to wait for them to get better before you can start to feel joy, happiness and love. You are free to begin working on **YOU** by making small, meaningful changes whenever **YOU** want to.

> **'When you finally learn that a person's behaviour has more to do with their own internal struggle than it ever did with you.'**

PROJECT ME

What actions would you like to take in order to start working on you? Write your answers in the box below, along with reasons why you deserve to pursue them.

Are you able to identify the last time you felt significant and enough?

This could be a time where you redecorated your living room and felt very proud at what you had achieved, adding final touches such as pictures, etc. Maybe you made an effort to lose weight, and found when you got on the scales that you had lost seven pounds.

_____

When was the last time you felt truly relaxed, and not like you were walking on eggshells? Do you feel anxious or tense before the addict in your life walks through the door, perhaps because you don't know what sort of mood they're going to be in?

Write down all the emotions you feel during the course of the day.

STANDARDS AND BOUNDARIES

When caring for and loving an addict, you must have standards and set boundaries in order to demonstrate that you're not prepared to accept their ways. This will also help to prevent them from abusing your love and taking advantage of your kindness, which they may see as a sign of weakness.

Personal boundaries are guidelines, rules or limits that a person creates as a means of establishing reasonable, safe and permissible forms of interaction. If you do not set clearly-defined standards and boundaries, you will soon slip into accepting the behaviours and attitudes of the addict, resulting in a quality of life that is far below what you deserve. It starts with falling into old patterns and habits, often beginning with the food and drink that you consume, before eventually informing the ways that you interact with people.

Standards and boundaries give clarity to others, making them a key starting point on the journey towards loving yourself. They will protect you from unexpected and unnecessary harm or disappointment, and you will gain more respect from the people around you as they become aware of, and learn to respect, the boundaries you have set. Over time, you will begin to feel better about both yourself and your life as your sense of agency increases.

In the chaos of addiction, the setting of boundaries plays an important role in assuring your own well-being while, hopefully, encouraging your addicted loved one to seek help. Common boundaries include: not allowing the addict to drink or use drugs around you, setting curfews, and refusing to bail them out of legal or finance trouble. It is important that once you set a boundary, you follow through on it, as the addict will see no reason to change if there are no consequences for not following the rules. Although setting boundaries may be tough and even seems harsh at times, it will go a long way towards teaching your addicted loved one to become accountable for their actions.

This is where you start working on YOU!

Start by asking yourself the following questions:

_____

1. What are you prepared to tolerate in your life?

    _____

    _____

    _____

2. What do you accept as reasonable behaviour?

    _____

    _____

    _____

3. What will make you feel significant?

    _____

    _____

    _____

4. What are you prepared to let go of?

    _____

    _____

    _____

5. What are your core values?

    _____

    _____

    _____

And remember the following key points:

- You can't change others, so change yourself instead.

- Decide the consequences of negative actions ahead of time.

- Let your behaviour, not your words, speak for you.

- Make self-care a priority.

- Seek support.

Once you put these standards into practise and resolve to stand firm in your beliefs and values, everything else will begin to fall into place. This is your chance to step up and put YOU first by raising the bar higher for yourself.

You will now start to see the life you can live, and be able to start working towards the life you deserve!

THE MAGIC QUESTION

Ask yourself the Magic Question: are you truly living the life you desire?

It is important to understand that you may be just as **addicted** to your enabling behaviours as the addict in your life is to their addiction and their manipulations.

In much the same way that addicts use drugs, alcohol and other addictive behaviours to avoid dealing with their shame or feelings of being unworthy and unlovable, you may be focussing on the addict's behaviour in order to avoid having to come to terms with your own issues. Your enabling behaviours towards the addict may be helping you to stay busy and distracted, allowing you to avoid having to confront the lonely, empty feelings that you are holding inside.

Although it may be scary to think about giving up behaviours that have formed your **'comfort zone,' is it not even scarier to think that you could end up living with them forever?**

THE MAGIC QUESTION

Part 2

TAKING ACTION

Uncomfortable action

Too many people mistake the practise of healthy self-care and putting themselves first for selfishness, even though selfishness basically means wanting what you want when you want it (stamping your feet), and being willing to step on whomever you have to in order to get it. This actually sounds more like the behaviour of an addict, and the truth is that if you try to take care of someone else before taking care of yourself, you will simply find yourself depleted and exhausted.

Self-care means respecting yourself enough to take good care of yourself in healthy and holistic ways, such as making sure that your physical, mental, emotional and spiritual needs are met. As an adult, it is your job to determine what your needs are, as you are the only one responsible for meeting them.

> 'Start over, my darling; be brave enough
> to find the life you want and courageous
> enough to chase it. Then, start over and love
> yourself the way you were always meant to.'

TAKING ACTION

Unfortunately, we don't always have the confidence to move forward and take action – there have been many times where this has been the case for me – so how do we gain the confidence to do something that we have never done before?

We can borrow confidence from past experiences, or from others we see leading the types of lives that we'd like for ourselves, and we can also have hope. Hope is strength and desire; hope is a belief that it will happen, and hope allows us to approach problems strategically, with a belief that we will achieve a goal. So, go ahead and feel hopeful; have the confidence to believe and trust in the universe to deliver whatever help is needed. You have to believe in yourself before anybody else is going to believe in you, so think of it this way: if you don't know where you're going, how do you expect to get there?

Trying to build a life you love without a clear vision of what you want will have you going around in circles, causing you to settle for less than your true self.

Don't forget, low self-confidence isn't a life sentence. Confidence can be learned, practised and mastered, just like any other skill.

It starts with daily practise, and although you may need to fake it before you make it at first, you will eventually come to believe it, and then the confidence will flow through you. As you begin to feel it more and more, others will start admiring and saying **'YES'** to you with greater frequency. You will also notice how the addict in your life becomes wary of crossing the line, as the standards and boundaries that you have set are acknowledged and respected.

TAKING ACTION

Tips for building confidence

1. Stay away from negativity; take a positive from a negative.
2. Change your body language and image.
3. Start to change those negative thoughts and voices in your head, and don't accept the words that an addict is saying to you. It's all about action.
4. Start being more prepared.
5. Start stepping out of your comfort zone.

Sometimes, your subconscious mind may be saying, *It's not the right time*, or your inner voice could start shouting, *We are alright where we are; let's not risk it. Let's stay here and hope we can fix him / her, and it will all be OK.*

In a crisis, we often go into fight or flight mode (we have two options), and this is the time to start pivoting from negative thoughts to positive ones. We can either stay and hope for the best, or start taking action. Just remember, there's nothing wrong with feeling uncertain and scared, as this is your life we are talking about after all.

Stop and think, are you facing some of these issues?

Are you happy?

Is your career or business suffering?

Are the children being affected?

Do you want this addict to be a role model for your children?

Do you want a better life? If you don't start shifting your thoughts and enable yourself to live the life that you deserve, you are going to end up settling for less than what you desire.

How do you pivot your thoughts? **Just remember, your best thinking got you here.**

This is your time; this is the right time, and you are going to start taking action and stop being abused and manipulated into enabling the addict for an easier life.

Following someone else's life plan and expecting it to work for you can often be destructive.

No more complaining to friends and family. No more being held back. No more being left without money. No more dreading what sort of mood they are going to come home in. No more having to tell the children to be quiet or good, due to you worrying about the addict's reaction to them.

Are you going to take back control of your life?

Next-level thinking. Next-level action. Next-level implementation

What is next-level thinking?

- Make plans for yourself (where you are going to live? How to get your finances in order. Who do you need to inform?).
- Visualise your goals (new house, new job, new car, new business ventures, freedom, stability, etc).
- How will you achieve these goals? ('I will start to x;' 'I will stop doing x;' 'I will need to be someone who is x,').

- Do you really want this situation to continue for the rest of your life (being consumed, bullied and abused)?
- Is your health being affected (low self-esteem, depression, lack of motivation)?
- Are your relationships with friends and family being affected (lack of contact / not seeing others)?
- Create a *For and Against* list.
- You want a happier life?
- You want the freedom?
- You want a better life for your children?
- You want to fulfil some of those dreams you have put on hold?
- You want more money?

What is the next-level action to take?

- Start looking for your own accommodation.
- Contact the Department for Work and Pensions if you need financial support.
- Approach family for support.
- Build / repair relationships with old friends and estranged family members.
- Keep moving towards your goals.

What is next-level implementation?

- Have you started to put your plans into action?
- Have you started to change your circumstances?
- Are you working on yourself?
- Are you making all of your aims become a reality?

> **Don't just read the advice in this book and say, 'Yeah, I will do that,' and then do nothing. Really work to get your shit together, and start to make yours the life that you truly want and deserve.**

TAKING ACTION

Setting goals ahead of taking action

1. List three steps you will take in the next week to get you closer to your goal:

   1. _____
   _____
   _____

   2. _____
   _____
   _____

   3. _____
   _____
   _____

2. List three steps you will take in the next month to get you closer to your goal:

   1. _____
   _____
   _____

   2. _____
   _____
   _____

   3. _____
   _____
   _____

Uncomfortable action

Sometimes, we have to take uncomfortable, imperfect action, even when we don't have the confidence to move forward. We can't always just switch confidence on, and so sometimes the action has to come first.

It is similar to the experience of starting a new job, where you're not sure how the system works until you start using it yourself. Over time, your confidence grows as you get used to the role, until eventually it becomes second nature.

We have to adopt and adapt; we have to flex our courage muscle, because courage is something you use when you walk in to the pub where the addict is drinking, after you have been summoned to pick them up, and you're not sure what kind of reception you will receive.

Courage is taking the addict to a meeting in the hope they will wake up and smell the coffee, and then seek professional help and support.

It takes courage to love and care for an addict, and that same courage is now needed if you're to decide where you want to be in **your** life.

You have two options, the first being scared, uncertain and frozen, and the second being ready to seize opportunity and begin focussing on **YOU**!

Start taking uncomfortable, courageous action, as this will pivot you in a direction that leads to the kind of life that you desire and deserve.

The key is to not be afraid. You may believe that there is no way you could ever afford to leave your addiction-marked relationship, but you are smarter and more resourceful than you realise, and solutions will present themselves. There is a limitless number of ideas that you just haven't had yet.

Possibly the worst year that you will ever experience in your lifetime

I am sure that during Covid-19, which has been a very worrying and stressful time even for those in relationships that do not carry the added strain of addiction, your eyes have been opened to many areas in life that you now realise were being neglected. You may now be more aware of how you have been enabling and accepting the behaviour of an addict due to them being around you more.

This may be the time where you decide that enough is enough, and start putting things into place ahead of taking action. Perhaps you have realised that you had previously just been going through the motions with the addict, putting your own life on hold because you're living the addict's life, giving them your time, money and energy, and being held back.

Maybe you have woken up and realised that **NO**, this is not who you are or what you want for yourself. There is more out there for you; you are meant to do and be more. You deserve more, because you have the potential to reach a much higher level of self-worth.

So, let's start by focussing on what it is that you want out of life, and work on the mindset you'll need in order to take the sort of uncomfortable and courageous action that will get you moving in a different direction.

TAKING ACTION

People often agonise over deciding when is the right time to take decisive action, such as leaving an addicted spouse. The truth is that there may never be a perfect time; you may just have to do it. It all depends on the individual circumstances of any given situation, although there are some universal signs that indicate when it's time to seriously consider leaving:

- Verbal or physical abuse towards anyone in the family, including you.
- Using drugs and / or alcohol in front of any family member (especially children).
- Refusal to seek help.
- Stealing from family members, or others, to feed an addiction.
- Constant drama and negative turmoil being created in the lives of family members or friends due to substance abuse.

I was 40 when I took action over my addicted ex-husband, and started working on myself and the life I deserved and wanted to create. I realised how my business was suffering; I couldn't concentrate – I was on antidepressants that kept me in a bubble – people were looking to me for guidance and support, but how could I advise or offer support if I wasn't practising what I preached? I then had a light-bulb moment and said enough. That was when I decided that I had to make changes by taking action and wrestling back control of my life, and so I threw away my antidepressants (always get advice from your GP before doing this) and left (this was the right decision for me).

You can regain control of your life, too. All it takes are small steps towards where you want to be, where you won't be consumed by the addict, and before you know it you will have started to overcome those feelings of low confidence, lack of self-esteem and courage, and even the guilt of not being able to fix the addict. You will finally come to realise that their problems are not yours, as you learn to overcome the obstacles that you have been putting in your own way.

Remember, where you are now is not permanent!

Start to shift away from those negative thoughts, and turn your back on the self-doubt that has been plaguing your mind. I can tell you from experience that when you take decisive action, it isn't long before you're feeling the wind beneath your wings.

Have you ever looked at your phone or TV and found it looks fuzzy, only for it to become clearer once you point the aerial in a different direction? That's what it's like when you alter your thinking, as you start to have those 'Aha!' moments in response to making even the smallest changes.

Sometimes, in order to recover from a relationship with an addicted person, it is necessary to leave in search of the time and space needed to assess what life could be like without addiction and its many consequences. In some cases, detaching also serves as a wakeup call to the addict themselves, alerting them to the damage caused by their addictive behaviours and encouraging them to seek help.

Leaving an addicted loved one need not be a permanent arrangement. It could simply be a way to stop yourself from participating in the addiction cycle by removing your enabling behaviours, which may involve bringing home a bottle of alcohol in order to avoid a fight.

'No more "I can't." it's all about "I can!"'

TAKING ACTION

What is your present focus, and what goals have you been putting off, or putting on hold, up until now? How will you go about putting measures in place to get you heading in the right direction? Are you focussing on yourself or the addict?

Loving and caring for an addict is both heart-breaking and soul-destroying, as your own life goes on hold while you try to fix theirs. Eventually, as you approach rock bottom, you begin to realise that it's you who needs fixing, as you have totally lost yourself in the addict.

You're worth more than just settling for an addict. If the relationship is constantly hard work, and nothing about it feels natural or light, with the addict struggling to show affection or even be considerate towards you, perhaps it is simply not meant to be. You deserve someone's best, so don't settle for anything less.

Do you really want change?

I know that you want to take action and start working on you, otherwise you wouldn't be reading this book! I know that you want this more than anything, and I'm here to tell you that you can make it a reality if you do just one thing for yourself. You are probably thinking, *If I can fix them (the addict) and work on myself, we can start to have a normal life*, but the truth of the matter is that you **CANNOT** fix them. The addict has to fix themselves, so start thinking of yourself first and foremost, a bit like putting your own oxygen mask on before helping others on a plane.

'It is not the external situation that is causing your suffering. It is your thoughts about the situation that are causing your suffering.'

I believe that you are ready for change and willing to take action. You have wasted enough of your time being consumed by an addict, acting as a co-dependent, and you have finally realised that all the promises the addict makes about how they will change are hollow and empty. I believe that you want to start living the life you desire and deserve, free from all responsibility for another's attitudes and manipulations, and that you can achieve everything you want if you commit to working on you.

Your safety and well-being first

First and foremost, I am just going to put this out there, as I would never be able to live with myself if I didn't.

If you are in a physically abusive relationship, the first action you should take is to leave the addict, as remaining could end up landing you in hospital – if it hasn't already – or worse. There are organisations that will guide you through accessing support for yourself and (if applicable) your children. Everything else we can work on together, but your immediate physical well-being should be placed in the hands of dedicated professionals:

safeline.org.uk
safelives.org.uk

You are at breaking point

1. You're just starting your own recovery.

2. You haven't done a ton of self-care or self-work yet.

3. You have been focussing on them and their addiction.

TAKING ACTION

4. You are not sure where to start.

5. You are not sure what the future will hold, but you're not necessarily thinking about that just yet anyway.

6. You're ready to be happy again; to laugh, have fun and be who you used to be.

7. You are ready to let go of old habits that may be hurting you and your partner.

8. You are ready to learn new ways of being in your relationship that will work for both you and your partner (if you chose to stay).

9. You are ready to put in hard work, which you know will pay off in the long run.

10. You are contemplating leaving the addict.

'You love them, and you don't want to leave. You have tried everything to get them sober and / or clean, but nothing is working.'

Imagine feeling peace of mind about your future, rediscovering (or discovering for the first time) your courage and confidence, and having a major breakthrough in your relationship with yourself. It doesn't matter if you stay or leave, or whether or not they get sober or clean; **it's all about you now!**

Do you ever feel like you are on a rollercoaster? Do you ever get frustrated, angry, sad or hurt? Now is the time to really get going and working on you. Trust in me when I say that you do deserve to be happy and to live a life of abundance.

TAKING ACTION

You were not born to nursemaid someone with an addiction while neglecting to take care of yourself.

Tools you can start to use

- Are you in the habit of overthinking things?
- Do you procrastinate?
- Are you a pessimist?

Develop a routine for each day. Start by adding new habits designed to work on you, eg you could start the day with journaling (writing your thoughts down).

If you have important matters to attend to, try to prioritise them early in the morning before doing anything else. This will help make the rest of the day seem easier.

There will be days where you feel emotionally low, or you are confronted with having to do something that you don't want to do (this is especially important to remember when it's an enabling act for the addict).

If you don't remind yourself every day about what you need to focus on and why you are taking action, it becomes easy to slip back towards old ways and listen to negative thoughts. This will lead to you procrastinating again.

Create a mood board and use it to stick up pictures of what you want to achieve. Put it somewhere visible in order to keep you focussed and visualising.

'Focus more on the "how to" and less on the "what ifs."'

If your thoughts start spinning as you are thinking about taking action, in your mind shout, **STOP!** Don't allow yourself to get stuck in the negative spiral of analysis paralysis.

Overthinking tends to become a way of trying to control things that you cannot control. This may cause you to miss out on the one thing that you really want to do, as you end up feeling too scared to take action.

Traits and knowledge

Start opening your mind to what you **can** do, instead of fixating on all the things that you can't do and what could go wrong. We need to reprogramme your mindset to reflect the fact that you're moving on from loving and caring for an addict, as let's face it, a lot of addicts are narcissists, or at least have some narcissistic traits. Addicts / narcissists manipulate to get their own way, sometimes by gaslighting you into believing that it's your fault they drank or used again, because they would not have done it if you had not said or done what you did. It's never the addict's fault; always yours or someone / something else's. Believe me when I say that **it's not your fault, it's theirs!**

> 'The toxic monster you saw in the end is who they really are. Never doubt your judgement just because they've decided to play nice.'

Most people recover once they leave an addict or start working on themselves, as they begin to figure out the addict's traits and learn ways to handle and disarm them. In this instance, knowledge is very much power, and you need to gather as much of it as possible in order to break free and bring yourself back to reality. It is this knowledge that will allow you to move on and rebuild your life anew, and recalibrate your mindset to think and feel for yourself; to ask your dreams to show you whatever it is that you truly want from life.

It is hard to fight your enemy if the addict is your parent(s), as you have been conditioned to think and feel a certain way about them for a long period of time.

It is also hard to fight your enemy if it is your partner, especially if you have only recently finished sleeping with them, as they have conditioned your mind and they know all of your weaknesses.

The only way to fight your enemy is to step out of the ring and leave them to do their own damage, allowing them to fail while you work on your true inner self by engaging in positive self-talk and resetting your mind.

When you have high hopes and dreams, but life just isn't working out the way that you want it to, it can be soul-crushing, especially if you're also dealing with a narcissistic addict. Most addicts will up their game in response to you finally standing up for yourself, as they hate losing control of someone else's mind, which only reinforces the fact that the problem is not you, it's them.

If you have spent a lot of your life around addicts, you already know that they make their problems yours. It does not have to be that way, though; you can walk free and leave them to fight against themselves. Yes, this can be very difficult to do, especially if you and the addict have children together, as can breaking away from family, due to the ingrained belief that family is most important. Thus, it is so vital that you reprogramme your mindset to allow you to fight these battles with calm, rational thought. You cannot fight emotionally, as you will inevitably lose sight of the fact that you cannot fix an addict.

If there are children involved, it is your responsibility to stand up and fight for them, ensuring that they have a stable routine. In the event of divorce proceedings, make sure that all correspondence takes place in writing, ideally by email (tip: set-up a new email account dedicated solely to dealing with the addict, so that you don't have to keep looking at their messages over and over again), and keep any examples of abusive language as evidence in case needed in court. Make sure that your sent emails only contain essential information, and refrain from getting angry and responding inappropriately, as we know that addicts like to push buttons to get a rise.

Even if you have been abused and conditioned over the course of many years, do not despair. You can always retrain your mind to think and feel how you want it to, as you decide where you want your life to take you.

It's time to stop feeling frustrated and upset, and obsessing over why these unfortunate things keep happening to you. Asking yourself why you can't fix the addict will only hold you back, and so you need to take all the energy that you've been putting into them and redirect it towards fixing yourself. Start thinking, *What can I do for me?*

Your mind is the key to success in recovery. To start creating a new life for yourself, you must start taking action today.

Talking to and preparing the children

Some of you may not have children, but before you think about skipping this part because it does not apply to you, **STOP!** Just hold your horses, as you may still benefit from what I believe is transferable advice on boundaries, bonding and monitoring.

Do you have a mother, father, niece, nephew, sister, brother or cousin that are trapped in an abusive, addicted relationship? Maybe you used to live in the household, before you were old enough to get away. It may be possible for you to support them with advice and guidance.

For those who do have children, no matter what age, this will be incredibly important to you, as I am sure that you will be able to relate.

When you love and care for an addict, you may be ambitious in terms of what you think can be achieved on their behalf. However, when it comes to handling the children and attempting to manage their interactions with the addict, it can be very difficult to figure out how best to protect them from mood swings and unpredictable, sometimes even abusive behaviour.

It may be with the best intentions that you say to yourself, *Let me just fix your dad / mum, and everything will be OK. All of our problems will go away, we will be a happy family and life will be good. Your daddy / mummy will be around for you.* You may want to believe that they will suddenly start showing up to football matches and dance shows, and taking part in activities; helping with homework or even taking an interest in university studies. You may have grandchildren whose lives you would like to take part in, perhaps wishing to have them stay overnight, but you cannot chance it due to the addict's unpredictability. Children often act as further motivation to fix an addict, in a desperate attempt at keeping the family together, but in time you will realise that they can't be fixed with or without children. Unfortunately, the addict does not share your outlook on life, as they are totally consumed by their addiction, which means that neither you nor the children will ever be their priority.

You should be putting your energy into the children, talking to and educating them about addiction, especially if they are still living under the same roof as the addict. Our children rely on us to raise, mentor and bond with them; to teach them right from wrong and always offer them safety, but these responsibilities are overlooked when all of our time is poured into an addict.

If you are currently in a relationship with an addict, I would strongly recommend that you take an honest look at your situation. Is it really what you want?

> **'When your children desire to talk to you and share their problems with you, stop everything and listen to them. There is nothing more IMPORTANT than them.'**

Look in the mirror and ask yourself, *Where is all my energy going?* Is it going towards fixing, solving, loving and trying to make better a person who is struggling with addiction, or is it going towards you and / or your children? We do not always know what we are doing while we are in a relationship with an addict, as we can't see the woods for the trees when we are just trying to get through each day. There is no reason to judge someone for making a poor choice, but we should strive to learn from our mistakes and make better choices in the future.

TAKING ACTION

There's every chance that you have been in this relationship for years, with the addict drinking, using drugs or repeating addictive behaviour, and you reacting in the same old ways. That's OK, because from now on, you are going to break this cycle and create new patterns, as you stop giving your energy to the addict and start focussing on you and your children.

What I am about to tell you may sound like I am trying to separate your family. You may read it and think, *Wait, are you telling me to get divorced / leave? Are you telling me that it would be better to take my kids and remove them from the addict's environment?*

It's just as well that you saw it coming, because that's exactly what I'm telling you to do. If there is drug-taking, alcoholism, fighting or smoking anything of any sort going on in your house, this automatically designates it an unsafe place for children, full stop. It is that simple; it is that cut and dry. Your children deserve to have a place in the world where they can feel loved, relaxed, monitored and bonded to you, with very clear boundaries.

> **'Not having any type of substances being used at home is a very obvious boundary that all of us have the right to, particularly children.'**

If you are telling yourself that your children are too young to understand what is happening around them, believe me when I say – and this is something I can guarantee – they know that *something* is going on. Children are like sponges, absorbing everything that they see and hear, and if they witness one parent verbally abusing the other, or they themselves bear the brunt of the abuse, it can be emotionally scarring.

TAKING ACTION

A child may not understand that the addict is also bipolar, or why they are spending a lot of time looking at the computer late at night, but while the specifics of a situation are often beyond their grasp, they are intuitive enough to sense that something is amiss. They understand that one parent is upset, and they pick up on it when the addict is slurring their words, just as they know not to expect to see them at football practise or dance lessons. They notice when a parent looks dishevelled or stops cooking like they used to, and they internalise the chaotic scenes that become their normal.

If you are not communicating with your children regarding addiction and the reality of their life, no matter their age or how painful it is to hear, you are only preventing them from understanding why things are the way that they are. I know that you love your children dearly; that all you want is to be a good parent. I also know that the last thing you want is for them to feel unsafe or unloved, or to think that it is somehow their fault.

'As parents, it is our job to be our children's biggest advocates. If we don't do it, who will?'

Your children's safety and future are in your hands, and it is up to you to protect them from your addicted partner.

What's written above will seem harsh and probably stings a little, and you may be tempted to stop reading here, but at the same time you know it's true, and the truth often hurts.

You must understand that I am not trying to hurt you, as I know that you are already hurt enough, nor am I looking to point the finger. What I am trying to do is give you loving truths, and I ask that you please be assured that I am **not judging** you, because I used to be you.

TAKING ACTION

I really do empathise with how you're feeling. For years, I allowed my children to share a house with an addict. My ex-husband even tried growing his own marijuana plants (he was not addicted to this particular drug, but rather to the money it could bring in) in our upstairs bathroom – we could smell it – and the children were breathing in the residue. Luckily, we also had a downstairs bathroom, but there were still plenty of occasions where the children would ask what was in the one upstairs, and they would be told to shut up and stop being nosy. I'm pretty certain that I used to feel sleepy from the fumes, so what was it doing to their developing brains? The fact that they were spoken to the way that they were is disgusting in and of itself, and although I was glad when the plants eventually died, it had the knock-on effect of making my ex-husband very angry and moody for weeks on end, which meant we all were walking on eggshells around him. The most annoying part was, I could not even tell my children why their dad was being such an arse!

For me, that was when enough was enough; I couldn't do it anymore. I didn't care if I was penniless, if I had no friends or if I had to go and live in a shelter. I honestly did not care what anyone thought, including my parents, siblings and friends. I could no longer allow my children to grow up in that kind of environment, where they were at risk of developing major addictions of their own if I didn't get them out.

Looking back now, and knowing that I did the right thing, I often ask myself, *Why did I put all that energy into somebody who did not want it?* It left me feeling guilty towards my children for a very long time.

'65% of children who start drinking at the age of 13 will become dependent or use.'

TAKING ACTION

Removing your children from an environment of addiction is so incredibly important to their future, as is talking to them about the effects of addiction, and having the guts to say (and it does take guts, make no mistake about it) that you are drawing a line in the sand; this is your boundary.

You must resolve to turn the trajectory of addiction around on its face, and refuse to let the cycle repeat with your children. They will be faced with enough temptation once they are out in the world, and so the last thing they need is to have addiction normalised at home.

If the addict shows no signs of admitting that they have a problem, and if they are not willing to seek help and support – eg staying in a dedicated programme for longer than 12 months – you need to start thinking about a contingency plan to get your children out of that house, no matter how old they are.

Your children need you to be a role model for them; to show them what it looks like to stand up for yourself and your future; to stand up to addiction and say, 'I don't need to deal with this anymore!'

'You do not need addiction in your life.'

You can and you will do so much better without addiction in your life. You can be incredibly happy without having to constantly deal with the chaos and trauma that addiction brings.

So yes, I am telling you to consider the idea of breaking your family apart, as this may actually be better for your children in the long run. Chances are that they will blame you for it; they may cry and yell. In fact, I almost guarantee that this will be the case, but in the end they will be grateful for it, because they are going to realise the benefits of living in a calm, stable environment. It may take many years, but I can assure you that they will eventually come to understand and appreciate what you did for them.

For those of you who do not have children, the need to separate yourself from the addict may seem less pressing, as the only person suffering is you, but you are just as deserving of a better life – of freedom, happiness and room to breathe – as anyone else.

Unfortunately, children of addicts are more at risk of being genetically predisposed to addiction than others, regardless of their environment. I myself am in this position, and so on my website (visionanddreams.co.uk) you'll find a programme designed for children to complete. As caring, loving parents, we all want to help our children and reduce the risk of them falling into addiction, and it is so important to educate them on the issue.

'As the parent, educate your children on the dangers of addiction.'

On a more positive note, if your children reach the age of 21 without smoking or abusing alcohol / illegal drugs, this usually means that they won't ever fall into those traps.

Educating your children is key to developing their knowledge and understanding of addiction. We cannot help our addicted partners, but our children are within our sphere of control. This is where we are powerful; this is where we have incredible opportunities to change the trajectory of our children's lives, and through them our grandchildren's and the many generations' beyond.

My children, who are now adults with families of their own, often say to me that one of the greatest gifts we have is that all of us come to the dinner table with different opinions. This started when I left my ex-husband, as I made a conscious decision to always allow them to voice their opinions and never tried to convince them that they were wrong. As a result, they have learned how to communicate effectively, arguing with one another with respect and kindness, all the while keeping an open mind.

When I was growing up, I never knew what it was like to communicate freely with my parents, as they were too consumed with their own issues and addictions, and I was left to my own devices. That's why I used to attract the wrong types of relationships; because of my limiting believes about myself and the relationships I could have. I have since done all the necessary work on myself, practising what I preach to others, and now I live a happy, fulfilled life, enjoying a great relationship with my children.

> **'The work we do as parents matters.
> Not only in the immediate future, but
> also in terms of our lasting legacies.'**

It is never, ever too late to start bonding with, loving and supporting your children, even if you think that you made a mistake by not removing them from an abusive environment. Remember, it is never too late to change anything in your life.

Be kind to yourself; love how you view yourself as a parent, and take the energy that you have been wasting on the addict and put it towards the people who need you most.

Clarity

- We have blind spots.
- We always start with what we don't want. What about what you do want?
- How do we become who we are?
- Why do we attract certain types of people in our lives?
- We can overthink.
- We do the things that we think about.
- Our problems only exist within ourselves.
- The way you view the world comes from the way you feel about the world.

A lack of clarity in life may be a result of not receiving enough encouragement as a child, denying you the space to be creative, to be motivated to try new things and to problem-solve without fear of failure. It is important to know that if something doesn't work out, this doesn't mean that there is something wrong with you. Most of the time, it's simply a case of taking a step back and trying something new. As I have been saying throughout this book, you can always retrain your brain to adapt to different methods.

Think of examples where you have felt resistant, restricted or lacking in confidence. Were you born with the idea or belief that was holding you back? The answer is **no**, you learned it, which means that if you are unhappy with your lot in life, you can just as easily unlearn your limiting thought habits. Start turning your beliefs around by taking control of your world, training your mind consciously until believing in yourself becomes an unconscious act.

Remember, it took us longer than a week to learn to walk, talk or even eat. You probably picked up a few knocks from falling over while trying to walk, and you'll have eaten plenty of food that you didn't like at first. Be aware that retraining your mind is going to take commitment, determination and motivation. You may stumble at the first new thought, and your first new action may not be much of a success, but so what? You have the rest of your life to learn what works best for you.

You will soon start to understand that life's problems are merely constructs of the mind, formed out of the things we have been told, and reinforced by the patterns and schemas that we have received from parents, teachers and peers, who might have all done their best at the time, but whose influence may need to be undone if you're to live the life that you want and deserve. If you can't do it on your own, seek out support (my details can be found at the back of the book). This is your life, so chase your dreams and follow through on your plans to catch them. This is not a dress rehearsal.

'The first time you put up with abuse, you're a victim. The second time, you're a volunteer.'

Signs of mental and emotional abuse

- **Character assassination:** This usually involves the word 'always.' You're always late, wrong, screwing up, disagreeable, etc. Basically, you're not a good person.

- **Shouting:** Shouting, screaming and swearing are meant to intimidate you, and to make you feel small and inconsequential. They may be accompanied by fist-pounding or throwing things.

- **Patronising:** eg, 'I know you try, but this is just beyond your understanding.'

- **Joking:** The jokes may have some truth to them, or be a complete fabrication. Either way, they make you look and feel stupid.

- **Insulting your appearance:** They tell you , just as you are about to walk out the door, that your hair looks a mess, your dress is too revealing or your makeup is too much and makes you look like a clown. These are just a few examples.

- **Belittling your accomplishments:** The addict / abuser may tell you that your achievements mean nothing, your qualifications will get you nowhere, your cooking is rubbish, etc.

- **Threats:** They will take the children if you leave them, or scar your face so that no other person will look at you, or leave you with no money / take the family home.

- **Monitoring your whereabouts:** They want to know where you are at all times, and insist that you respond to their calls, texts or emails immediately. They may turn up at your workplace or business with no warning, just to check that you are there.

- **Unpredictability:** They may explode out of nowhere in rage and anger, shower you with affection or become dark and moody at any given time, leaving you feeling as though you are walking on eggshells.

- **Jealousy:** They accuse you of cheating and flirting, or of talking and texting on the phone. They feel jealousy if you dress up to go out, or even if you put on makeup to go to work, accusing you of meeting someone or having an affair.

- **Blame:** Whatever is wrong in the addict / abuser's life is entirely your fault. You are not supportive enough, did not do enough or interfered when you shouldn't have.

- **Destroying and denying:** They may do things to your belongings, such as break your phone or hide your car keys, and then deny all of it.

- **Shutting down communication:** They will ignore you by blanking your attempts at communication, whether by telephone or text, or even in person.

- **Withholding affection:** They may refuse to touch you; not even holding your hand or patting you on the shoulder. They may refuse sexual relations in order to punish you, or they may get you to carry out something that makes you feel really uncomfortable.

- **Isolating you:** They try to turn your family against you, perhaps by making things up about you not wanting to see them. They may tell your friends that you have been saying insulting things about them behind their backs, or try to make you think that no one likes you and that you are going crazy.

> **'These behaviours reflect the addict's own insecurities. They want to create a hierarchy in which they're at the top and you're at the bottom.'**

Emotional neglect and isolation

Addicts will tend to place their own emotional needs ahead of others', and many will try to come between you and the people who are supportive of you, as a means of making you more dependent on them and them alone. They may do this by demanding respect, calling you needy or disputing your feelings.

Am I co-dependent?

A co-dependent relationship may be defined as a situation where everything you do is in reaction to the addict's behaviour. They need you to boost their self-esteem, and you have forgotten how to be any other way. It is a vicious circle of unhealthy behaviour.

When you are in a relationship with an otherwise good person who happens to be suffering from addiction, you just want them to get better. You want a normal life with them, and you believe that you could have this if they were only free of their addiction. Of course, you're not mean or needy or a nag; you just want to kick this illness out of your home once and for all, so that you can have the life you've always wanted with your loved one.

Co-dependency can be harmful when we feel entirely responsible for helping an addict. We need to stop blaming ourselves for this illness, which we did not cause and we certainly cannot cure. Sometimes, the best way to help an addict is to let them fall apart and say nothing; no unsolicited advice, no shaming and no saying 'I told you so' (this can be so hard to do). Just listen with a compassionate heart, and keep quiet.

TAKING ACTION

Signs of co-dependency

- Poor self-esteem.
- Relying on your partner for your happiness and self-worth.
- Difficulty communicating your desires and needs.

Co-dependent behaviour is described as a reliance on somebody else for confidence, validation and self-worth. It may manifest as a person requiring permission for their own wants and desires.

Co-dependency is not inherited, and under the right circumstances and with the right people it can be your greatest gift, but you must learn to recognise where and when it is acceptable, and find confidence and courage within yourself in situations where it is not safe to be co-dependent.

Co-dependent tendencies may develop if you are exposed to a relationship where addiction, abuse or trauma take place. They can often be traced back to childhood, but may also begin later in life.

Letting them suffer the natural consequences of their addiction

When they get caught telling lies to their boss, do not cover for them.

When they can't remember where they have left their keys after having too much to drink, don't feel as though you have to run around the house searching for them.

If they get done for speeding or caught on their mobile phone while driving, do not take their points for them because they may lose their licence.

Not bailing them out and letting them suffer the natural consequences of their actions is one of the best ways to force an addict to confront the destructive nature of their illness and behaviour. You're smart enough to learn when to use your gift of co-dependency for good, rather than trying to leverage it into controlling and fixing the addict.

Talking to the in-laws

- Do you feel the need to talk to your in-laws, so that they know and understand the truth?
- You may have a great relationship with your in-laws, and do not want to ruin it by talking to them about your partner.
- Will they believe you?
- Will they accept what you are telling them?
- Will they blame you?
- Do they enable your partner?
- Do they know, but simply refuse to acknowledge the issue?

Going to the in-laws about the addict can often be very daunting. After all, it is their child you are talking about, no matter what age they are.

You feel as though you need to speak the truth because no one else is willing to do it, and that's assuming they even realise there is addiction involved. You do not want to seem like you're being disrespectful, but if it serves your heart and your soul and brings you peace, you should share what is happening with your in-laws and family members. Give them information about your loved one's addiction freely, but make sure that you have your expectations in check while doing so.

When I finally spoke to my in-laws, I had left my ex-husband for the second time – or was it the third? I can't remember! – and no one had any idea what I had been dealing with, as it had never been brought up; or, if they did know, they did a good job of hiding it. I knew that my ex-husband would make it sound like everything was my fault; he never took responsibility for anything, so I wanted to put them straight and try to avoid them thinking poorly of me.

I had a great relationship with them; had a lot of time for them and spent a lot of time with them. There were various things that went through my mind: *They are both elderly* (in their 80s), *so what if they don't understand? What if it makes them ill, or worse, as his dad's health is not great. How much do I share?* In the end, I took the bull by the horn and just went there, knocked on the front door and received a warm welcome from his mum. She made me a cup of coffee, we sat down and I began...

I explained that I had been dealing with their son, who is a drug addict, and that I could no longer cope with his controlling, abusive ways. I said that I had given it my best shot, had tried everything I could think of to get him clean, and that I hoped they would understand. I understood if they felt anger towards me, but I was clear that unless he got the help and support he needed, I would not be going back to him. I added that I didn't believe his addiction was a reflection of their parenting, and that there was no blame being placed on them.

They were understandably shocked and devastated, but I have to say that they were both very understanding and supportive towards me in that moment. Other parents may not be quite as willing to accept the truth about their addicted son or daughter, so backing yourself up with hard, indisputable facts may be a good idea.

'The power of denial is so incredibly strong.'

Afterwards, I told my ex-husband that I had been to see his parents, and that I had explained everything to them. I was extremely worried about what his reaction would be, but he actually seemed glad that I had told them, as he was then able to get some support and guidance as a result. However, he only did this because it was what others wanted for him – he did not decide it for himself – and although I did go back to him once he made a real effort to change, it wasn't long before the addiction cycle started again.

What happens when in-laws think that you are partly to blame for their child's addiction?

Addicts often come from families in denial, which is tantamount to enabling, because these are parents who have been unwilling to enforce extreme consequences for poor decisions around addiction.

This is obviously a generalisation – it's not the case with every addict's family – but when it comes to approaching your in-laws, it's important to consider the possibility that they already know or suspect that something is going on. After all, if they were in denial before you met their son or daughter, what makes you think that they are not going to be the same way now?

TAKING ACTION

Go in with the expectation that they will continue to exhibit the same old behaviour patterns, and realise that what you are telling them probably isn't going to change their stance. This can be a really difficult pill to swallow, as not only do you want their support, but you also find it impossible to believe that they, as caring parents, could stand by and watch their child sink into addiction. You may be wondering why are they not shocked and angry enough to intervene, if not for you or their child then at least for their grandchildren?

Difficult though it may be, try putting yourself in their shoes for a moment. Besides, staying mad at them is not going to help your cause, so you may as well learn to forgive. It's also worth remembering that If you feel you cannot approach your in-laws face to face, writing a letter may also help you in the process of your healing.

A parent's greatest fear is losing a child, and chances are that they are terribly afraid of confronting a disease that is often fatal. Some parents will choose to bury their heads in the sand, or even worse, blame you for their child's issues, so please bear all of this mind once you feel ready to make your case.

There are three solutions to every problem:

Accept it, change it or leave it.

If you can't accept it, change it.

If you can't change it, leave it.

When you pay the in-laws a visit, or if they come to you, say something along the lines of, 'I just want to enlighten you because I feel like it is important that we are all on the same page. I want you to understand the truth and severity of the

TAKING ACTION

situation. I am not here to blame or point fingers, nor do I wish to make anyone feel bad. I only want to bring light to the truth, so that we can come to terms with what we are dealing with.'

Opening the conversation this way will automatically cause defences to drop, as you will have established that you are not blaming them or anyone else. You will have also made it clear that you are not looking to throw the addict under the bus, even though they may often do just that to you, because you are the bigger person here. If the family then chooses to continue to deny the truth and / or blames you, take this as a sign that it is not going to work, and stop wasting your time trying to convince them that there is a problem.

I understand how frustrating and upsetting it can be to have in-laws that are not supportive of your efforts, but here is the truth: you are incredibly smart, and you are already working on you and your new mindset by taking action and implementing plans. If you are following the advice given in this book, you are beginning to realise that you do not need anyone else to agree with your assessment of the addict or to authorise your decision to leave. You only need to trust in your own judgement; it is not your job to convince your in-laws of anything.

Time reveals lots of things, and that is all you need. When I left my ex-husband, I did maintain some contact with my former in-laws, but after a year or so it became less and less frequent. The children eventually reached an age where they could make their own way to their grandparents' house, and so in the end I lost contact with them altogether. As for my ex-husband, he fell apart, hit rock bottom and is now pulling the same kind of stuff with his family that he once did with me.

TAKING ACTION

For you, it may be the case that approaching the addict's family brings you closer to them, as they may actually understand what you have been going through and offer the necessary support.

Time

In time, you will learn to be proud of yourself for leaving without anyone else's approval. It will be liberating, you will feel empowered and you will realise that it was **YOU** who took control of the situation and won back your own freedom.

Don't be afraid to lose people; be afraid of losing yourself by trying to please everyone around you. When you are being mentally and emotionally abused, trust your instincts. Know that what you're going through is not right, and that you are under no obligation to live in fear.

Leaving the relationship is usually more complex if you are married, have children or share assets, and you should always seek legal advice if this is your situation. These are not, however, excuses for you to stay.

Give yourself time to heal, reach out to supportive friends and family members, or seek more professional, accredited means of support at visionanddreams.co.uk.

Self-care involves finding acceptance in yourself, and recognising exactly where you are on your journey. Have the confidence to confide in others, and trust in your divine plan

'Loving someone unconditionally
does not mean unconditionally
accepting destructive behaviour.'

You are going to be telling a different story very soon, a story of how miracles have found you; one filled with so much inspiration. You will give so much hope to so many others when they see how much you overcame on your journey to become your best self.

Five things to quit

1. Trying to please everyone.

2. Fearing change.

3. Living in the past.

4. Putting yourself down.

5. Overthinking.

**'The most reliable way to predict
the future is to create it.'**

PART 3

LEARNING TO FLY

'Next time someone makes you feel unworthy, simply smile and say, "I hope you find what you are looking for."'

Now is the time for you to start pursuing whatever it is that you truly want from life, eg a new job, travel, time with family, home renovation, a different car, a new business venture, etc. Make a list of things that you really want to achieve and start working towards making them happen, ticking each one off as you go.

Life is so short, but you have already started to come through the worst of it and now is your time. You are no longer consumed by the addict, and you are becoming stronger each day as you rediscover yourself through the process of self-care. Never let anyone hold you back, put you down or say that it won't work. If they are truly worthy of you, they will encourage and support you to fly, so just go for it!

Ask yourself if what you're doing today is getting you closer to where you want to be tomorrow, and do everything in your power to ensure that the answer to this question is **YES!**

Remember, even the smallest steps in the right direction are examples of progress. Divorce is OK, breakups are OK, starting over is OK, moving on is OK, being alone is OK... but what is not OK is staying in a place where you are not valued or appreciated.

'Are you ever truly living if you're
not really comfortable?'

Three actions you can take right away to start shifting your mindset and your results:

- Focus on something you really want.
- Make a committed decision.
- Increase your awareness.

'Be proud of who you are and
how well you are doing.'

Grieving

Leaving the addict and starting fresh may be a daunting prospect, I get that. Think of it this way, though: you are finally about to embark on your true path.

You may be feeling intense emotions that will often override logic or explanation, as all breakups carry a fundamental feeling of rejection. This just means that you need to be consistent with your self-care, which is crucial to your healing.

As time passes, you will go through all of the emotions associated with grief, since a loss is a loss regardless of whether or not your partner was an addict or an abuser. The fact remains that you became accustomed to a certain way of life, and so a period of adjustment is required.

Some of the emotions that you will most definitely feel are anger, anxiety and sadness, and then possibly depression, too, before eventually acceptance. No one can give you a time frame for how long any of these emotional periods will last, but by constantly working on yourself and utilising the coping strategies described in this book, such as mental effort, meditation, exercise (be it breathing, physical or both), intention setting, affirmations, gratitude and planning, you will continue to make progress until the healing is complete.

The good news is, you are well on your way towards freedom and the life you deserve.

You will grieve in your own way, doing whatever feels best for you, but here are some suggestions based on past experiences:

- **Take some time off.** Try not to suppress your emotions, especially in the immediate aftermath of leaving the addict, as you might have been denying your true feelings for some time out of fear of upsetting them. Around two weeks after I left my ex-husband, I drove up and down the road one evening just screaming my head off, and I have to say that while some of what I came out with was obscene (I was not even consciously aware that I knew some of those words), it still felt amazing. Taking time off will give you the opportunity to sob and scream, if that's what you feel like doing.

- **Listen to sad music.** You're probably thinking that I have lost the plot, as I hear you say, 'Sad music? Surely, I need to avoid it?' However, emotive music will bring up and reinforce painful memories, while also normalising the grief you are feeling and reminding you that these feelings occur in us all.

- **Talk.** Talking to supportive people, be they friends, family or colleagues, is great, although they may have a limited understanding of what it's like to be consumed by an addict, in which case professional help may be more appropriate. You may come to recognise deep-seated patterns of behaviour or thinking within yourself, which could be causing you to end up in addicted or abusive relationships.

- **Reading books.** Seeing what you are going through described on a page is sometimes calming in a way that can't be matched, as it reassures you that you are not alone.

- **Sleep, eat and exercise.** Tempting though it may be to just stay in bed and abandon your usual routine (I know that Bridget Jones duvet time, complete with ice cream and a romantic movie, seems just the medicine you need), it is crucial to maintain some normality at a time like this, and let's face it, you have already wasted enough time on the addict, and you have a new life to live. Going to the gym or attending an exercise class will help release pent-up anger and / or energy, while walking in the park and getting in touch with nature – hug a tree, take a book and lose yourself in the outdoors – is great. Meditate and visualise your future, seeing how wonderful all of your new experiences are going to be. Visit the friends you have not seen for a long time, and start rebuilding bridges with them if necessary. Try going for a swim to take your mind off things, even if it is only for half an hour, and take a walk along the beach, listening to the waves, which I find to be truly amazing for freeing the mind (this is my go-to during difficult times).

- **Treat yourself.** Purchasing some new makeup or treating yourself to a new pair of shoes may seem like unnecessary splurges, but on this occasion, as a one-off boost to your self-esteem, it is very much allowed. Don't see it as a licence to max out the credit card, though, as that would defeat the object, and I'd also delay any decisions on drastic changes to your hair for at least three-six months, lest you make a rash decision that you end up regretting.

- **Meet new people.** When you feel ready (usually three-six months), start testing the dating waters. The key here is to take it slow and steady, but if you have been doing the necessary self-care, don't procrastinate. It's all about getting back in the saddle, as they say, so even if you do not yet desire another intimate relationship, there are plenty of platonic activities that will help you to build trust in another person.

- **Set firm boundaries.** One of the worse possible outcomes following a breakup is an on-off, ambiguous limbo relationship developing, as this almost always leads to worsening heartache. It is advisable to wrap up loose ends and discuss important unresolved issues with your ex as soon as possible. Discussing child access, maintenance and the splitting of joint assets, etc is important. If this can be done amicably, great, but if there has been physical abuse in the relationship, it will have to be done through a solicitor. You should refrain from contact with the addict as much as possible, to prevent them pulling on your heart strings and offering empty promises, and if they do not respect these boundaries and become threatening, abusive or even stalk you, you should go to the police and get a restraining order (keep a log of the dates, times and nature of each contact). Having been consumed by an addict, you now have to go through a withdrawal period. It can be quite easy to be tempted to go back, as they try to convince you that they are finally going to change by getting help and support, while making no end of empty promises. If you feel the urge to go back, just remember what life was like with the abuse, the constant let-downs and the lack of money due to the financial strain of addiction, not to mention the staying out all night, and then turning up the next day stinking of stale booze and cigarette smoke. Don't forget how you and / or the children were never top of the addict's list of priorities, which led to all those dinners being thrown in the bin because they were too busy taking cocaine or having affairs. The choice is, of course, yours alone to make, but just ask yourself if going back means being true to yourself and / or your children?

- **Social media blackout.** Taking time out from social media is essential, especially if you are connected with the addict. Unfollow and unfriend your ex, so that seeing them does not slow down your healing process. Avoid the urge to post those passive aggressive memes you have saved, and start surrounding yourself with lots of laughing, smiling people. Having friends around you can help you to feel supported and cared for, and don't be afraid to take a trip or go on a spar day / long weekend.

Who are you?

Over the course of your relationship with the addict, you will have gradually lost touch with your true self. This might have been a result of the things that they told you about their past relationships, and what they perceived to have happened, which led you to change in order to earn their trust by proving that you are not like their previous partners. You might have lost your confidence and suffered diminished self-esteem due to the addict's constant abuse and putdowns, making you feel intimidated and scared, but you are now able to wake up to why their ex-partners either cheated on them or left.

It could be that the addict was your first partner, and so, having no experience of a normal relationship, you did not know any different, even though your gut feeling was that how you were being treated was wrong. Whatever the case, now that you have made a conscious decision to leave – or stay, if that's your choice – and you have made a commitment to self-care, you have started to become stronger again.

- Who were **you** before the addict?
- Who do **you** want to be?
- What were **your** hobbies and interests?
- What would **you** really like to achieve?

Take the lists you have made during our journey through the book and start pursuing your greatest ambitions, as you now have the freedom to be yourself. Start today with the first item on the list, and put plans in place to make it a reality.

The first thing on my list was starting **Visions & Dreams**, as I wanted to offer others the kind of support that I could never find for myself. I had been to many support groups seeking help with the addicts in my life, but I just knew that there was more to be done for those of us living in the shadow of someone else's addiction, and so that's where my journey into business began. I studied and trained, learning how to occupy and thus understand the mind of an addict, which involved taking various courses in order to gain the necessary qualifications, although I maintain that nothing beats life experience. Obviously, I am not knocking the efficacy of those courses, as they did provide me with more context and clarity in regard to the position I was in, while also opening my eyes to what was happening in my own relationship. I never needed to speak to a therapist, though, as I plotted my own healing journey.

'The path forward is easier to follow when you know where you want to go.'

For many, popular culture has inculcated the idea that love and romance should come easily, and so they end up blaming themselves when this doesn't turn out to be the case. In the real world, breaking up makes you discover more about yourself and learn more about what you want through experience of what doesn't work for you.

Remember, leaving the addict has given you an opportunity that will only be squandered if you slip into doubt and self-abuse. Take stock of what you have learned about yourself, and this will enable you to grow until you are ready to find a suitable long-term match.

'In the process of letting go, you will lose many things from the past, but you will also find yourself.'

You may be prone to chastising yourself for perceived faults in your personality, your appearance or things you've said (or didn't say), so as soon as you find yourself starting down this slippery slope, get to writing in your journal and repeating your affirmations, sources of gratitude and positive intentions. Write about everything you have learned about yourself through self-care, and what you want to work on in the future. This could include:

- Communication skills.
- Discovering hobbies.
- Learning to trust in yourself.
- Beating procrastination.
- Loving yourself first.
- Establishing and maintaining standards.
- Putting boundaries in place.

There will soon come a day where you will marvel at how far you have progressed. You will know your true worth, and you will see how much you have achieved. Grieving serves the purpose of helping you to be more ready for your future, when you wake up one morning after a good night's sleep and, realising how great you actually feel, notice that the pain and heartache has gone. For the first time in a long time, the addict will not be the first thing on your mind.

Saying YES!

Start saying **'YES!'** to everything.

- Do you want to go away on holiday? Say **'YES!'** and book yourself a spar weekend, or maybe a holiday in the sun, soaking up vitamin D with a good self-help book (I can recommend one).

- Do you want to go see that show you've been talking about? Say **'YES!'** and purchase the tickets.

- Haven't you always wanted to take dance lessons? Say **'YES!'** and book in at a dance club (this is a good way to meet new people, too).

- Do you want to get fitter, and / or change your eating habits to lose some weight? Say **'YES!'** and book an appointment with a nutritionist (ahem, perhaps me). You do not have to join a gym, as you can walk, jog or even do exercise classes online, although having a gym membership is good for motivation, as well as meeting new people.

Alcohol and having Fun

Enjoying alcohol may seem impossible right now, especially if you are still raw after leaving an alcoholic, but getting out and having fun does wonders for the brain by reducing anger and increasing positivity. It turns out that laughter really is the best medicine, as it releases endorphins, which are your body's natural mood elevators, while at the same time increasing pain tolerance.

I am certainly not recommending that you go out drinking to excess all the time, as this can be a slippery slope towards depression (alcohol is a suppressant), and although drinking may temporarily dull the pain, those feelings will still be there waiting for you when you wake up the next morning, and with the added hindrance of a hangover. Drinking will also be detrimental to any weight-loss ambitions you may have.

Always remember:

**Grapes must be crushed to make wine,
Diamonds form under pressure,
Olives are pressed to release oil,
Seeds grow in darkness...**

**Whenever you feel crushed, under
pressure, pressed, or in darkness,
you're actually in a powerful place.**

I really want you to start realising all the things that you are, and to believe in what you are working towards. I want you to read this section every day for 90 days, until it fully sinks in. Make it a part of your daily routine, along with journaling, affirmations and gratitude. When you repeat something long enough, you do start to believe it.

Read the following every day:

- I am strong
- I am brave
- I am kind
- I am beautiful inside and out
- I am an inspiration
- I am powerful
- I am loved
- I love with all my heart
- I am giving
- I am special
- I am unique
- I am determined
- I am courageous
- I am funny
- I am a giver of smiles
- I am an amazing person
- I am caring
- I am perceptive
- I am generous
- I am a wonderful soul
- I am a good person
- I am a fantastic friend
- I am well
- I am fit
- I am healthy
- I am **ALIVE**

'Delete the energy vampires from your life; clean out all the negativity; build a team around you that frees you to fly; remove anything toxic and cherish simplicity.'

Mementos

Clinging onto treasured gifts from your ex, or looking at old photographs of the two of you together, will only hold you back from healing and moving on. You may even find that having them around triggers feelings of sadness, loneliness or anger, and so I would suggest deleting all such photos from your phone, to prevent the urge to keep looking at them. Any framed photos should be either box up and thrown out, or handed over to your ex. However, I do understand that if you have children, you may want to keep a couple of family photographs for their benefit, but I would avoid having them out on display unless it is in the children's own bedrooms.

If some items are too nice or valuable to throw out, consider donating them to charity, as this comes with the added bonus of knowing that you are making a positive difference to someone else's life.

There may also be an urge to go out and slash your ex's tyres, key their car or post abusive messages to their social media accounts, especially if they have started a new relationship. You must remember, though, that it will only be a matter of time before their new partner sees the true nature of their addiction, and obsessing over feelings of being replaced will only keep you locked in the past. Besides, the feeling of satisfaction that comes with acts of retribution is very short-lived, and the addict is not worth the hassle of legal consequences.

Forgive and Forget

Once you are able to forgive the addict for everything that happened between you, and all that you have gone through, the forgetting can start. This is the natural cycle, and it's worth remembering that forgiveness is something you do for yourself, not the other person.

Start thinking about what it is that you want to forgive, recalling how it made you feel and tracing where your thoughts take you. During these periods of reflection, ask yourself:

- What can I learn from this?
- Would I do things differently?
- What warning signs will I look for in the future?
- How will I use these experiences to grow?

Forgiving is not the same as excusing bad behaviour, nor does it require reconciliation. You are not implying that it was OK to abuse you the way that they did; you're simply letting go of the burden of anger, because forgiveness is freedom.

Remember, you cannot control how others act. The only thing you can control is **YOU**.

Tell yourself that you forgive the addict for their actions and mistakes, but be mindful of the fact that it can sometimes take a long time for feelings of resentment to subside. For me, the process of rediscovery brought with it a lesson about acceptance, as I resolved not to be bitter about the years wasted or resources squandered on the addict. In the end, all I could do was learn from the experience.

Embracing life

Start enjoying your life. It's good to move on and embrace who you are as an individual, so take this opportunity to spend more time with the people in your life who really matter. Sit back, relax and tell yourself, *I have got this*, because you really have.

Never hold onto the past, lest you run the risk of letting it define your future.

Warnings

Remaining friends is a big no-no if you are still romantically attached to the addict, especially if you still harbour ideas that you could fix them or you are worried that something may happen to them. Accepting that the relationship is over has to be the very first step taken after leaving, otherwise it will be almost impossible for you to truly move on.

If you want to remain friends with the addict, I advise that you do not pursue this for at least a year or two, allowing for any lingering romantic feelings to be fully extinguished. Going down the 'friends with benefits' route is never a good idea, either. This will do nothing but hinder your individual progress, while at the same time allowing the addict to keep using you as an enabler. As a guide, perhaps consider cutting off all contact until you are happily dating someone else.

My true feelings

If I did not have the courage and strength to take my life back, moving past the guilt and anger that I had caused with my poor decisions, chances are that I would still be tangled up in my old tendencies to this day. Instead, I decided to recognise those experiences for what they were and put them to good use in my life.

I could have easily remained the same person, carrying my long-standing behaviour into other situations and relationships, but I chose to move on. I know that a few people thought I would end up going back, which is understandable, as that's exactly what I'd done on several occasions before, but I was sincere in my wish to affect positive change.

It was not the easiest road, but in the long run it allowed me to be me, and to live the life that I truly wanted and deserved. Now, I am happy and free. I no longer carry the weight of someone else's addiction on my shoulders.

Each and every day, I meditate, visualise and repeat my affirmations and sources of gratitude. I also have my Archangel Michael cards, which I use to ask him questions in addition to seeking his general support and guidance, and he always has the answers I need (you may not be a believer, but this has worked for me on my journey towards learning how to believe in myself again). The coping strategies and tools that serve my needs may not be suitable for you, but that doesn't mean you won't be able to find some value in them as methods of focussing your self-care.

> 'If you can't fly, then run,
> If you can't run, then walk,
> If you can't walk, then crawl,
> But whatever you do,
> You have to keep moving forward.'
>
> – Martin Luther King Jr

LEARNING TO FLY

My mission is to empower and support others to achieve their **Visions & Dreams**.

I am passionate about guiding and supporting people to recognise their worth, realise their dreams and step into their own unique power to build a life that they truly deserve and love.

I hope that this book has brought you some clarity, or even an 'aha!' moment regarding your life with an addict. If you are looking for more guided support, please have a look at my offerings at visionanddreams.co.uk, or contact me at info@visionanddreams.co.uk to learn more about how we can work together to help you reach the life that you desire and deserve.

I have also created several guidance, support and encouragement programmes for anyone who has become addicted to an addict, details of which can found at the **Visions & Dreams** website.

GRATITUDE

While writing this book has been a solitary process, it was certainly not something I did entirely on my own. Numerous people have been there to support me throughout this endeavour, and I would like to acknowledge them here. I would also like to express my immense gratitude to my wonderful children, Danny, Alex and Ellie, for putting up with me during all that we have gone through. My children are my strength and my guiding lights, and I am incredibly thankful and proud that they are in my life.

I would like to thank the friends who were there for me throughout my whole journey of being **addicted to an addict**.

I would like to thank the witches for entering my life when it counted most. You know who you are!

GRATITUDE